Cream And Sugar

Kara Schneider

BookLeaf Publishing

India | USA | UK

Made with ❤ on the BookLeaf Publishing Platform
www.bookleafpub.in
www.bookleafpub.com

Dedication

To the lover girls who never learn,
and to the boys who forgot how to yearn—
this is for the ones who feel too much,
and for those who forgot how.

Preface

Love is messy. It's a quiet war, fought in the spaces
between longing and loss, between hope and heartbreak.
Coffee and Cream is not a story of perfect endings or
neatly tied bows. It's an ode to the raw, the unspoken,
and the unfinished.
This is for the lover girls who keep giving, even when it
costs them, and for the moments that linger long after
the people are gone. It's about the late-night texts you'll
never send, the coffee that grows cold on the counter,
and the memories that taste both bitter and sweet.
In these pages, you'll find fragments of what it means to
love and be loved, to ache and to mend, to break and
rebuild. These aren't lessons, but reflections—an
invitation to feel everything, unapologetically.
So take a deep breath, turn the page, and let's begin.

Acknowledgements

First and foremost, to the lover girls—this book exists because of you. Your stories, your heartbreaks, your resilience, and your unwavering belief in love, no matter how messy or painful, have been my greatest inspiration. To the late nights and early mornings, the caffeine-fueled hours spent turning thoughts into words, thank you for keeping me company. Coffee and cream weren't just the title—they were the lifeblood of this book.

To my friends and family who held space for me, even when I disappeared into my own head for days on end, thank you for your patience, your encouragement, and your love. You've been my steady ground when everything else felt like quicksand.

To the readers—those who see themselves in these pages and those who don't—thank you for picking up this book. Whether you're here to feel, to heal, or to escape, know that every word was written for you.

Finally, to love itself, in all its chaos and beauty: you're impossible, infuriating, and unforgettable. And somehow, you're always worth it.

1. The Type of Beautiful

I watch you from a distance you'll never cross,
a chasm carved by love and loss.
I don't belong in your orbit, I know,
but I stay, hoping my silence will show.

I wish I was the type of beautiful you'd see,
that your eyes would catch and never set free.
But I am the quiet, the unanswered call,
the flicker of light you don't notice at all.

I love you with the patience of unshed tears,
with the ache that's grown over quiet years.
You'll never know how my heart aligns,
how it beats to the rhythm of your careless signs

But your heart is a locked door I can't break,
and I am the ghost of a choice you won't make.
So I love you from here, a distant view,
wishing I was the type of beautiful for you.

2. Unclean

"Leave me.
I am unclean,
a vessel cracked, leaking poison.
I reek of ruin,
of sins I cannot wash away.
Touch me,
and you'll wear my filth forever.
I will cut you,
I will bleed into you,
and you will curse the day
you thought I was ever worth saving."

"No", he said, "tell me every terrible thing
you've ever done.
Spit your darkness at my feet,
let it seep into the earth beneath me.
Let your sins collide with mine,
and let me love you anyway.
Let me kiss the rot you hide,
slurping your confessions like holy water.

3. The Last-Minute Apology

I set the table, plates aligned,
hope flickered, soft and undefined.
Chose my outfit, checked the time,
a fragile smile—a fleeting rhyme.

The phone lights up, the message plain,
"Can't make it tonight, sorry again."
The weight of words sinks deep inside,
a quiet hurt I cannot hide.

I'll pour the wine for one, not two,
toast to the ghost of a night that flew.
Fold the napkins, dim the light,
wrap my heart up tight tonight.

4. Was it me, or the sky?

The idea of me is soft, almost pure,
a fleeting glow, something easy, obscure.
But up close, I'm sharp—I'm hunger, I'm ache,
a trembling thread that's too easy to break.

Is it the weight in my chest, the cracks in my voice?
The way I pull back like I don't have a choice?
What darkness in me made you step away?
What ghost in my eyes begged you not to stay?

I am raw, I am aching, I am hollow and bright,
a storm in the day, an ember at night.
If you need escape, I won't ask you why—
but the question will linger: *Is it me, or the sky?*

5. Untitled

I often think about the quote,
"I want to be loved so hard it hurts."
But love, when it arrives like a flood,
is a soft stitch over every wound.

We ache for a love that bends the bones,
that sets fire to shadows and silences ghosts.
It's not the kind of hurt that splits or bleeds,
not hunger, nor loss, nor desperate pleas.

So maybe it's not love that hurts at all—
it's the longing, the ache, the endless fall.
But once we land where love is bright,
No hurt survives, no fear can fight.

6. Loud

Please let me love you loudly—
let me roar with the colors you've carved into me.
A crest burned so deep into the mantel of my tapestry.

Let me taste your pain, let it ooze into my mouth.
We can stain the carpets and bleed paint into the walls
so when years pass our ghosts will mark these empty
halls.

7. A Princess Finally

Wishing to light the torch built from stones and decades of stories.
To have a world all our own, one touch would erase any other glory.
Where rain could thrash at our sides, and we'd giggle in the face of thunder.
All there'd be is our soaked clothes, and the terrified secrets we hide under.

Yearning to let each others warm gazes disarm all our hearts soldiers.
To ignite the flame, surrendering our beauty to its one true beholder.
Lingering on our breaths, scared to say the words that would make it real.
Looking into a mirror, and seeing a strangers smile that owns power to heal.

Staring at the jump below us, hearts in our throats, wishing to stay afloat.
But the slippery rocks could never sever that night and the words we wrote.
Our cottage would grow to be our castle, every straw sewn into gold.

A princess finally in treasured frames where
photographs never get old.

8. Coffee

In dim-lit rooms, the hours pass,
where dreams fade slow, like fogged-up glass.
No shouts, no screams—just quiet sighs,
a tethered heart, a gaze that lies.

The coffee cools in chipped white cups,
a clock ticks down, the daylight's flux,
each second slips, a silent plea,
for something more than just to be.

Hands folded tight, they feel the weight,
of small, unspoken shards of fate.
The life they thought was theirs to claim,
now worn and hollow, stripped of name.

And yet, they breathe, each breath a stone,
in walls they built to die alone.
A quiet life, in silent chains,
where desperation still remains.

9. Cream

It lingers, heavy, in my spoon's arc,
a pale apology for what's too dark.
But what can it mend, this fleeting gloss?
This cloak of sweetness over loss?

I've poured it in, again and again,
hoping it might dilute this pain.
But it's still there, beneath it all,
the bitter taste that fills the hall.

So I drink it down, this hollow gift,
the way we do when hearts still drift.
It cannot save me, it cannot redeem,
But still, I pour. I pour the cream.

10. Yearning to Unbecome

I used to gather beauty like rare shells,
each one nestled close,
hoping it might teach me
the language of the sea.

I wanted to be beautiful,
like the curve of moonlight,
softened by sky,
or roses that only whisper,
never bloom too wide.

But now I wish I could learn the art
of sinking away, the delicate erasure
of edges, the quiet drift into shadows
where my skin is just skin,
not story or invitation.

To drift free of curves,
to unlearn this softness,
to untangle the weight of gaze,
and become something boundless,
unmeasured, no longer a shape
to be held in someone else's eyes.

11. Right Person, Wrong Person

Right person, wrong time—a tragic refrain,
a love song played in the pouring rain.
Fingers nearly touch, then slip apart,
a fleeting chance, a fractured heart.

Wrong person, right time—just as cruel,
lessons learned in fate's twisted school.
Each glance a spark that always ignites,
a comedy staged in the dead of night.

The stars align, then scatter askew,
their promises fading in shades of blue.
"Was it ever meant to be, or just a tease?"
A whisper lost on a restless breeze.

12. The Fireplace

You are not the fire that scorches or burns—
you are the hearth where my flame returns.
When I flicker, your shelter, keeps me alive,
a steady place where my spark can survive.

I burn within you, and you burn in me,
two flames entwined, wild and free.
Not consuming, but feeding each other's glow,
a warmth that deepens with embers aglow.

In your quiet heat, I find my grace,
for love isn't fire—it's a fireplace.

13. Till The Rain Stops

Till the rain stops, kiss me softly,
in this warm embrace that feels almost lofty.
Clothes soaked through, yet our hearts ignite,
sheltered here in love's quiet light.

The rain drowns out the world beyond,
yet here we are, unbreakably bound.
Lean closer now, let my whispers trace,
the edges of your soul, in this tender space.

Every touch melts the cold away,
your hands, your warmth, make the moment stay.
Soft skin, trembling, in love's sweet refrain,
a timeless secret beneath the rain.

14. Becoming

I crave myself,
each scar, every curve,
a feast laid bare beneath trembling hands.
I ache to bite into the sinew of my worth,
consume the marrow of my doubts,
and lick the sweetness from my own wounds.

Let me swallow whole
the love I never sought,
gnaw on the bones of forgotten dreams,
and savor the pulse of my own becoming.
To hunger for me,
to be nourished by me—
a banquet where I am both hunger and cure,
the meal and the fire,
the teeth and the tongue.

15. Velvet

16

I'm not the velvet wrapped key you've been looking for,
but I loved you so much, I really tried to be more.
But I'm getting tired of this, my love, this war.
Struggling to string words together even for this
metaphor.

But I don't want to lie to myself and I don't want you to
be sad.
So please, please tell me how to become more, to add.

16. Never Get so Comfortable to Forget Your Umbrella

Painting on an illusion
of a toothy bright grin.
A perfect performance.
as the video ends.
But the curtain closes
and reality creeps back in.

My smile plummets down,
to my puddle of torment;
as quickly as the walls fell
of the home I felt was finally
permanent.

But did the roof actually
keep my head dry?
Those shingles of promises
were just a smoke screen,
if it was all just a lie.

But the air has cleared,
the dust has settled.

Taking my first steps
out of the ruins of pictures
into the rain clouds
that were always there.

Silently, cold and shaky,
gathering up my pride.
I am here again,
spreading my retired umbrella wide.

17. My Winter, My Spring

The petals you fell for, were only ones you wished to
pluck.
Wanting only to scrape the insides of my pollen with
your fingernails.
To put your hands on my softness.

My stems plead for me to make you stop,
but I pretend that my leaves don't need water.
Lying to myself that when it snows,
maybe you'd still look at me as if I was in Spring.

But you aren't the sun.
And I'm not what you really want.

But please, just for a few more minutes let me be craved.
Let me feel as if the bed that I grow in is one worth
laying in,
regardless of my season.

18. Twine

I will remember you always,
for you could see right through
to my leftovers that I tried to keep hidden
with string under my bed.

Scared that I'd get yelled at for the mess.
Soiling the blank canvas I was born with,
with beautiful ugly colors.

But you found my ratty twined package.
And instead of yanking your hand away,
you turned me over gently, examining
my wet marks and splotches.
Kissing slowly, one by one, the shame away.
Leaving brush strokes of color on my clutter.

Now when I wear my strings I wear them as ribbons.
Carrying yours and mine, a banner, forever

19. What's Left?

If I unspooled myself from the threads
of labels, likes, and accolades;
set aside my spine, my heart, my legs—
would there be anything that stays?

Strip me from the muscles I've earned,
from clever words and work well-spun,
detach each triumph, every turn—
what's left of me when all is gone?

Am I still whole without my parts,
without the things I do or my spark?
Would you still meet me in that space?
Where I am not my steps or my face.

20. Sugar

Your hands slithered around my waist, your chains
invisible,
brought me coffee with cream, your words were sugar.

But the coffee was never sweet, a truth so bitter.
Each sip was a lie, each glance was a splinter.

21. The Skin of a Fig

I was a house once,
plaster splitting off my wood ribs,
nails clawing out like secrets
wishing to tell anyone who'd listen.

And there was a time I was stone,
granite against the world.
Rivers tried to wear me down,
rushing with the rage of glaciers,
to dampen the curves of my
fire.
But my stone was not immune
to the relentless grind of time.
my surface smoothing with every injury,

Now I am velvet,
but not the kind you think—
I am not a ballroom curtain,
not red or lush.
No, I am the kind of velvet
that wraps figs, cloaking
the tender purple flesh beneath
a skin that bleeds sugar when bruised.

Touch me now.
Feel the silk that I have become.
But know—
I was not born this way.
I was carved.